Holiday & Everyday Projects

Table of Contents

Holiday Projects

Useful Crafts

WATERBIRD BOOKS
Columbus, Ohio

President:
Vincent F. Douglas

Publisher:
Tracey E. Dils

Project Editors:
Joanna Callihan,
Lindsay Ann Mizer

Art Director:
Robert Sanford

Interior Design and Production:
Christopher Fowler,
Suzanne Reinhart

McGraw Hill **Children's Publishing**

This edition published in the United States of America in 2003 by Waterbird Books,
an imprint of McGraw-Hill Children's Publishing,
a Division of The McGraw-Hill Companies
8787 Orion Place
Columbus, Ohio 43240-4027

www.MHkids.com

Library of Congress Cataloging-in-Publication Data is on file with the publisher.

Printed in the United States of America.

1-57768-528-8 (HC) 0-7696-3153-3 (PB)

1 2 3 4 5 6 7 8 9 10 PHXBK 09 08 07 06 05 04 03

The *McGraw·Hill* Companies

Using This Book

- After choosing a craft, check the list marked "What you'll need." These items are the art supplies and tools you will need to make the craft. Some materials are listed as "optional." That means that you can use them, but you do not need them for the craft. You might base your decision on whether you want a certain look or whether that item is readily available.

- The next thing you should do is read all the directions before you start the craft. You should also read the "Suggestion(s)," which might involve different tools or materials.

- Then, collect the materials and follow "Here's how" to make the craft.

Improving Cutting Skills

Some children who are still learning how to use scissors cannot seem to cut on the lines no matter how hard they try. This problem can often be fixed in a fun way. Check to see "who is in the driver's seat"; that is, check for correct finger placement. Correct finger placement involves the use of the thumb and the middle finger, not the index finger. The middle finger has more strength and maintains better control.

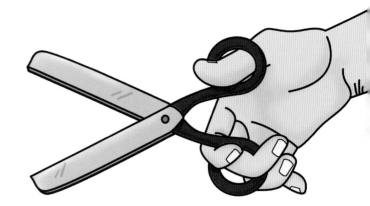

If the opening in the handle is large enough, both the index and middle fingers can be inserted. However, the index finger is only "going along for the ride." The thumb and the middle finger do all the work (driving).

If your child's fingers are too large for the scissors, he/she may need to readjust the grip and eliminate the use of the index finger when cutting.

Be ready to do any cutting for your child as needed. A younger child especially may need supervision. Don't let him/her get discouraged if you need to take over. Continue to provide your child with opportunities to practice cutting.

Painting Tips

Watercolor paints, the kind in a plastic, boxed palette, are used most often in this book. When tempera paint is used, you will find liquid tempera more convenient and easier to measure than the powdered form.

Some activities call for paint dishes. Pie pans or foam trays work well for these activities. However, it is recommended that you use clean foam trays from supermarket-packaged baked goods, fruits, or vegetables, because meat and poultry trays are difficult to disinfect. You can also mix paint in an ice cube tray or muffin tin.

The Color Wheel

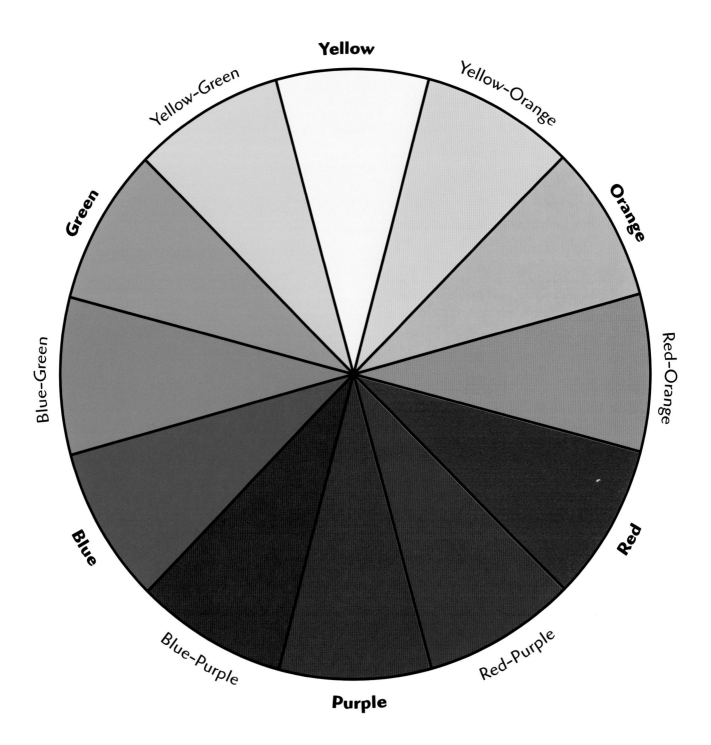

Holiday Projects

What would the holidays be without colorful decorations? Think of a plump Thanksgiving turkey, a ghoulish Halloween monster, or a bright red Valentine's Day heart. The Holiday Projects section features projects for many major American holidays. And by changing colors here and shapes there, you can make many of these crafts for different celebrations.

For example, the Halloween Pumpkin Lantern can be changed to look like Abraham Lincoln or Father Time. And you can make the Father's Day Planter into a gift for a grandparent or a friend. Let your imagination go wild! And have a happy holiday, too.

Gift Wrapping Decorations

Make these decorations instead of a bow when wrapping a gift. Or make them into ornaments to hang!

What you'll need

- ☐ construction paper in different colors
- ☐ ribbon, yarn, or string
- ☐ stapler
- ☐ glue or tape
- ☐ ruler
- ☐ scissors

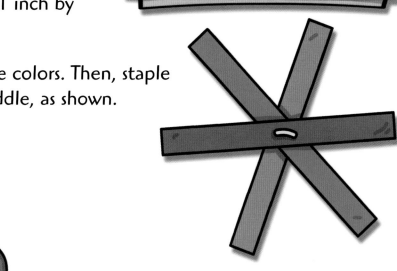

1. Cut construction paper into 1 inch by 12 inch strips.

2. Arrange the strips in alternate colors. Then, staple the strips together in the middle, as shown.

3. Create various designs by folding and gluing or curling the top and bottom ends of the stapled strips.

4. Use ribbons to attach them to holiday presents.

Suggestions

● Use these as ornaments on your Christmas tree.

● Use red and green paper for Christmas; blue and white for Hanukkah; red, black, and green for Kwanza.

● There are endless ways to fold the paper strips—use your imagination to make up your own.

7

Cookie Cutter Ornaments

These ornaments will be popular gifts—and they're lots of fun to make! They are perfect to add when gift-wrapping, instead of a bow.

What you'll need

- 2 cups flour
- 1 cup salt
- 2/3 cup water
- felt-tip pens
- cookie cutters
- glue
- ribbon
- paper clips
- photographs of you
- mixing bowl
- round cutting tool smaller than your picture
- wax paper (optional)
- rolling pin (optional)
- clear plastic spray, available in art supply stores (optional)
- an adult

1. The night before you do this project, make the following recipe in the mixing bowl: Mix the dry ingredients with your hands, then add water. Add more water as needed to create a mixture the texture of stiff pie dough.

2. The next day, roll out the dough with a rolling pin or pat it out to about 1/4 inch thick.

3. Cut out the dough with cookie cutters. Using the round cutting tool, cut a hole in the center of each shape.

4. Push a paper clip through the top of each shape for the hook.

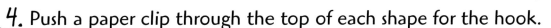

5. Let the shapes dry out for several days. It is best to keep them on wax paper.

6. When the shapes are dry, decorate them with felt-tip pens.

7. Have an adult help you spray the shapes with clear plastic spray, if desired.

8. Carefully place glue around the edges of the hole on the back of each shape.

9. Glue your photograph on the back of each shape. If the hole is larger than the photograph, glue your picture onto a piece of round paper, then glue the paper to the back of the shape.

10. Tie a ribbon around the paper clip to hang each ornament.

Fuzzy Valentine

This cuddly bear makes a great Valentine card to send a hug to someone special.

What you'll need

- [ ] brown and red construction paper
- [ ] brown and red yarn
- [ ] cardboard
- [ ] newspaper
- [ ] pencil
- [ ] scissors
- [ ] glue
- [ ] tempera paint
- [ ] construction paper scraps
- [ ] old paintbrush (optional)
- [ ] toothpick (optional)

Here's how . . .

1. Cover your working surface with newspaper.

2. Cut out a bear shape from the brown construction paper.

3. Glue the bear shape to the cardboard and cut it out.

4. Cut brown yarn pieces about 1/2 inch long.

5. Pull apart the strands of yarn, as shown.

6. With your finger or a brush, spread glue onto the bear's body and press the yarn into the glue. If desired, use a toothpick to press and guide the yarn. Do a small area at a time until the bear is covered.

7. Tie the red yarn around the bear's neck.

8. Cut out a large red heart and glue the bear on top of the heart.

9. Paint a message to your Valentine. Add a face with construction paper and yarn.

Patterned Shamrocks

Good luck will be with you when you cut and decorate these shamrocks on Saint Patrick's Day!

What you'll need

- ☐ cardboard
- ☐ drawing paper
- ☐ crayons or markers in shades of green
- ☐ pencil

1. Make at least two copies of the shamrock patterns below on cardboard and cut them out.

pattern

pattern

2. On the drawing paper, overlap the shamrocks and trace around their outlines with the pencil.

3. Color different designs within each shamrock.

Paper Maché Easter Egg

Everyone will want to know how you made this magical egg. It looks even better hanging in the sun!

What you'll need

- assorted colors of tissue paper
- balloon (round, not long)
- 1/2 cup flour
- salt (so the maché doesn't mold)
- 1 cup warm water
- paper clip
- yarn
- baking pan
- newspaper
- apron or old clothes
- pin, paper clip, or anything sharp to break the balloon

Here's how . . .

1. Cover your working surface with newspaper and wear an apron over your clothes.

2. Blow up the balloon part of the way and tie a knot in the end. Stick a paper clip through the knot.

3. Tear the tissue paper into strips or squares.

4. Combine flour, water, and salt in the baking pan. Mix it with your hands until it has a soupy consistency.

5. Dip a tissue paper strip into the mixture. Then, wrap it around the balloon.

6. Continue dipping and wrapping tissue paper, overlapping each one, until you have covered the balloon except for a hole the size of a quarter around the balloon's knot. You may want to add several layers around the balloon.

7. Let the balloon dry. This may take overnight to do.

8. Pop the balloon with the pin and pull it out using the paper clip in the knot.

9. Use the paper clip stuck through the opening and a piece of yarn or string to hang it. Hang your egg design from the ceiling or outside on an "Easter tree."

Eggshell Mosaic

Mosaics are pictures made up of small things like tiles or glass. Try this mosaic using dyed eggshells.

What you'll need

- ☐ dyed eggshells from Easter eggs
- ☐ poster board
- ☐ markers
- ☐ newspaper
- ☐ glue
- ☐ pencil

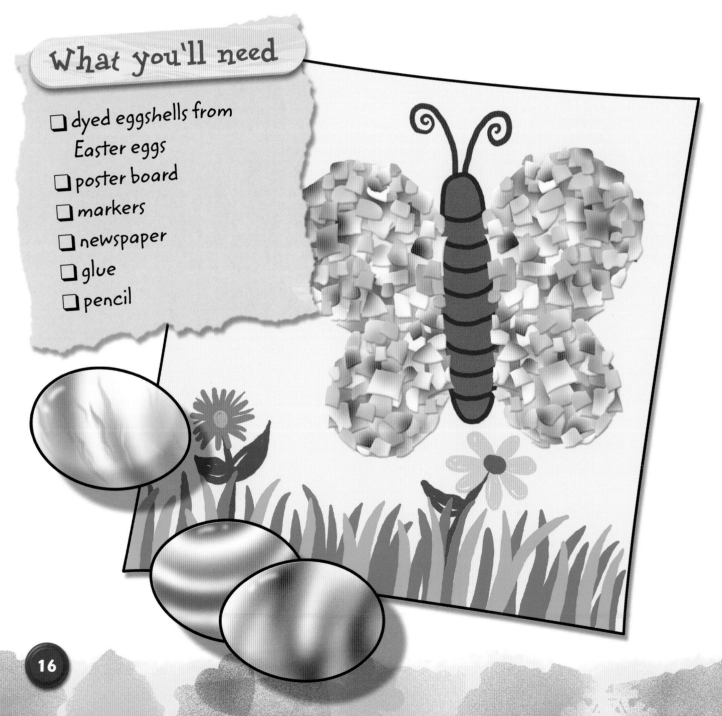

1. Cover your working surface with newspaper.

2. Crush the colored eggshells into small, but not tiny, pieces.

3. Using a pencil, draw a simple shape on a piece of poster board.

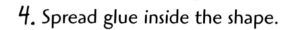

4. Spread glue inside the shape.

5. Sprinkle eggshells onto your glue shape. Let it dry, then shake off the extra shell pieces.

6. Color a background, if desired.

Suggestions

- Instead of sprinkling the shells, arrange them by color on your design.

- Use white eggshells instead of colored ones. Use watercolors to lightly paint the shells *after* you have completed your design.

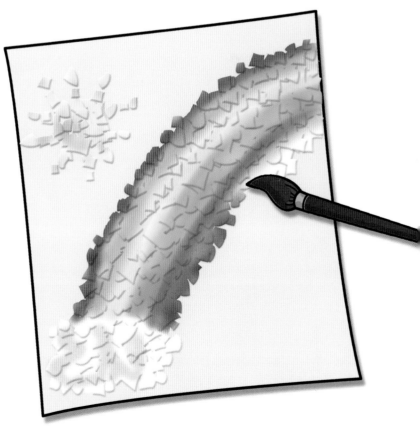

Mother's Day BoxCard

Mom will get a real surprise when she opens this box. It's a BoxCard!

What you'll need

- ☐ 9" x 12" light construction paper
- ☐ white construction paper
- ☐ crayons or markers
- ☐ scissors
- ☐ tape or glue

Here's how . . .

1. Make a larger copy of the box pattern on the right on light construction paper.

2. Cut out the box pattern along the outer solid lines.

3. Color the sides.

4. Fold in on all small dotted lines.

5. Tape the sides of the box together at the tabs.

6. Write a Mother's Day message on a long, narrow strip of the white paper.

7. Fold the strip like a fan, as shown.

8. Tape the end of the strip on the inside of the box.

9. Cut a slit in the top and close the box.

Suggestion

● Use this as a card for any holiday, including Father's Day or Grandparents' Day.

Father's Day Planter

Give Dad some grass he doesn't have to mow for Father's Day. Remember to start this in May!

What you'll need

- [ ] white foam drinking cup, large size
- [ ] potting soil
- [ ] rye grass seed
- [ ] 9" x 12" white construction paper
- [ ] crayons or markers
- [ ] scissors
- [ ] glue

Here's how . . .

1. Fill the cup 2/3 full with potting soil.

2. Sprinkle grass seed on top of the soil, then cover it with a thin layer of potting soil, as shown, and water.

3. Put the cup in a sunny place and water it every few days. It will take about 7 days for the grass to begin to grow and form the "hair" on the Father's Day Planter. Start the project 2–3 weeks before Father's Day to allow enough time for the grass to grow.

4. The day before you give this planter as a gift, color and cut out face parts from construction paper. Add features to make it look like your father!

5. Glue the face parts to the outside of the foam cup.

6. Be careful to keep it upright if you wrap this gift. A fancy gift bag would work best.

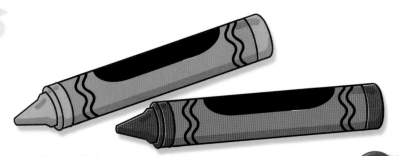

Fourth of July Fireworks

Make your own fireworks using paint, a straw, salt, and a little hot air!

What you'll need

- [ ] 12" x 18" black construction paper
- [ ] light red, white, and light blue tempera paint
- [ ] water
- [ ] salt
- [ ] plastic drinking straw
- [ ] paint dishes
- [ ] spoon

Here's how . . .

1. Thin some tempera with water to make it runny.

2. Use a spoon to place drops of the paint on the paper.

3. Hold the straw tilted and slightly above the paint. Blow from different directions to move the paint to create a starburst design. (Remember to always blow out—not suck in—through your straw when creating these paintings. The paint is great but not great tasting!)

4. Choose a different color and repeat the same procedure on another part of the paper. Designs can overlap.

5. Do the same thing using the third color.

6. While your painting is still wet, sprinkle it with salt. Gently shake off the extra salt after everything is dry.

paint

paint

Halloween Lantern

You can make this Halloween Lantern, or change the designs and hang it up for any holiday or party!

What you'll need

- [ ] 9" x 12" orange construction paper
- [ ] black construction paper
- [ ] scissors
- [ ] glue
- [ ] tape or stapler
- [ ] string or yarn
- [ ] ruler
- [ ] pencil
- [ ] paper hole punch
- [ ] orange and black crepe paper streamers (optional)

1. Fold the orange construction paper in half.

2. With a ruler, draw lines from the fold every inch, as shown. Stop 2 inches from the top.

3. Cut on the lines you have drawn.

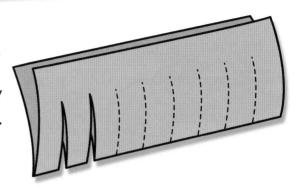

4. Unfold the paper and tape the ends of the lantern together.

5. Cut out the eyes, nose, and mouth for the pumpkin from black construction paper, then glue them to the lantern.

6. Glue on crepe paper streamers, if desired.

7. To hang your lantern, punch holes in the top and hang it with a string, as shown.

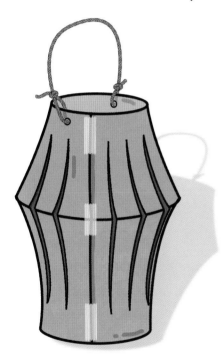

Suggestions

● Make a black lantern cat using black construction paper for the body. Add eyes, ears, nose, mouth, and whiskers.

● If you use crepe paper, make sure it doesn't get wet in the rain. The color will run.

Sweet Turkey

He may not be a turkey dinner exactly, but this turkey is still delicious.

What you'll need

- ☐ apple
- ☐ large marshmallow
- ☐ small colored marshmallows or gum drops
- ☐ 2 cloves or raisins
- ☐ toothpicks
- ☐ vegetable peeler
- ☐ carrot
- ☐ ice water
- ☐ an adult

1. Have an adult help you use the peeler to cut thin carrot strips. Put them in a glass of ice water. They will curl themselves after a few minutes. These will be side wings and the wattle.

2. Attach the large marshmallow to the apple with a toothpick to form the head.

3. Push the cloves into the head to form the eyes.

4. Attach the small marshmallows to the body with toothpicks to form the feathers, as shown.

5. Attach the side wings and wattle (curled carrot strips) to the body with toothpicks.

Face Mobile

The lightest breeze will bring your character to life! It's fun to make and fun to watch!

What you'll need

- ☐ two 9" paper plates
- ☐ scissors
- ☐ construction paper
- ☐ white thread
- ☐ white glue
- ☐ paper hole punch
- ☐ gummed loose-leaf reinforcement
- ☐ plastic curtain ring
- ☐ fiberfill, yarn, cotton, craft fur, or curled gift ribbon for hair

Here's how . . .

1. Carefully cut the centers from the paper plates so that the rims remain together, as shown.

2. Decide who or what your character is going to be. Cut ears, eyes, eyebrows, a nose, a mouth, cheeks, a hat, a tie, a mustache, or whatever you need for your character from construction paper. Make enough for 2 faces.

3. Position the construction paper parts inside one of the plate rims. Be sure the pieces are well-spaced so that your mobile will turn freely.

4. Measuring from the rim, cut lengths of thread long enough to join the parts.

5. Glue each set of parts together, sandwiching the thread between them. This is needed so each feature will be the same on both sides as it turns.
(continued on next page)

6. Put a small amount of glue around the outside of one rim. Place the other rim on top, matching the edges of both plates, as shown. Let it dry.

7. Glue hair and other features to your character.

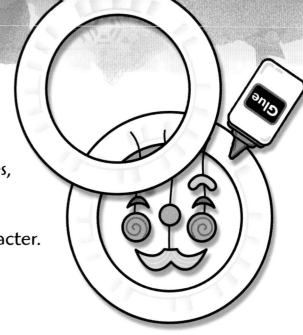

8. Punch a hole at the top center of the hat. Put a gummed reinforcement around the hole.

9. Tie a long thread from the hole to the curtain ring to make hanging your mobile easier.

Suggestions

● Have an adult use hot glue to make it last longer.

● Try your own characters.

Useful Crafts

The Useful Crafts section features objects you can really use. And once you've decorated them, these crafts will be more than useful—they'll look great, too.

In this section, you will find a variety of interesting projects, from bird feeders to bulletin boards. Many of the crafts are items you will want to use every day, such as the Mirror Plate or the Piggy Bank. And other projects, such as the Treasure Box, are excellent choices to give as gifts.

Use the crafts as suggested or make up your own uses for them. For example, you might use the Wind Sock to study weather patterns by watching the streamers for wind speed and direction. Be creative!

Pine Cone Bird Feeder

Fun to make and fun to watch, this natural bird feeder may become a favorite hangout for your feathered friends right outside your window!

What you'll need

- ☐ pine cone
- ☐ peanut butter
- ☐ birdseed or bread crumbs
- ☐ butter knife or spoon
- ☐ string

Here's how . . .

1. Tie the string around the pine cone.

2. Use the knife to spread peanut butter over the cone.

3. Roll the covered cone in birdseed or bread crumbs.

4. Hang the feeder outside near a window.

5. Watch to see who will eat from it.

Barrette Holder

You'll never wonder where your barrettes are after you make this fun Barrette Holder!

What you'll need

- [ ] two 9" paper plates
- [ ] crayons, felt-tip pens, watercolors, tempera or acrylic paints
- [ ] heavy rug yarn (about 1/2 skein)
- [ ] colored ribbons
- [ ] white glue
- [ ] yardstick
- [ ] scissors
- [ ] rubber bands

Here's how . . .

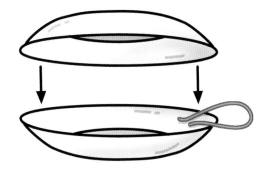

1. Loop a piece of yarn to be the hanger.

2. To make the head, glue the rims of the plates together with the eating sides facing each other, as shown. Glue the hanger between the two plates at the same time.

3. Color a face on one of the plates.

4. When dry, glue a few strands of yarn to the forehead to make bangs.

5. For braids, cut 18 strands of yarn, each 1 3/4 yards long.

6. About 5 inches from one end, secure the yarn with a rubber band.

7. Divide the yarn into three equal parts (6 strands each) and braid it. About 5 inches from the other end, secure it again with a rubber band.

8. To make two braids from the one long braid, tie a piece of yarn around the braid, midway from the ends.

9. Put glue on the rim of the face plate where the hair would be. Place the braids around the face.

10. Tie the ribbons over the rubber bands.

Suggestion

● Have an adult use hot glue to make it last longer.

Wind Sock

Make this Wind Sock out of your favorite colors! Hang it outside or use it as a decoration for your room.

What you'll need

- [ ] old window shade
- [ ] yarn
- [ ] paper clip
- [ ] crayons, markers, or paint
- [ ] glue or stapler
- [ ] scissors
- [ ] ruler
- [ ] paper hole punch
- [ ] crepe paper (optional)

1. Cut the window shade to be 6 inches by 18 inches. This will be the top strip.

2. Color the top strip with bright bold shapes.

3. Cut five strips from the shade to be 3 inches by 18 inches and glue them to the back of the top strip, as shown. Or use five strips of crepe paper.

4. Cut two strips of the shade to be 1/2 inch by 18 inches and glue them over the top strip to make it more sturdy.

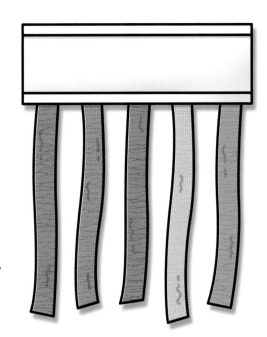

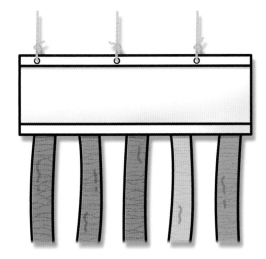

5. Use a ruler to place a dot at 1 inch, 7 inches, and 13 inches from the left edge of the top strip.

6. Punch out the dots with a hole punch.

7. Thread a piece of yarn through each hole and tie a knot to secure each piece, as shown.

8. Glue the ends of the top strip together.

9. Gather the yarn ends and tie one large loop or knot.

10. Open a paper clip to make a hook for hanging the wind sock, as shown.

Bulletin Board

Bulletin boards are perfect for displaying your favorite photos, school papers, and posters!

What you'll need

- ☐ foam board (or foam sheet)
- ☐ fabric
- ☐ tacks or stapler
- ☐ ribbon
- ☐ paper clip
- ☐ glue

List for sleepover:
- ✓ teddy bear
- ✓ pillow
- ✓ games

Josh and Sammie

Me

1. Cover the foam board with a piece of fabric large enough to cover the front and back.

2. Keep the fabric in place by using tacks to attach it on the back.

3. Glue the ribbon around the edge of the bulletin board for a border.

4. To make a hook, use a tack to fasten a large paper clip on the back.

Suggestion

● Decorate your board as much as you wish. You may want to add more to the border or your name to the board.

Piggy Bank

Saving money is fun when you can feed a happy pig in the process!

What you'll need

- ❑ 2 disposable soup bowls
- ❑ lightweight cardboard
- ❑ pipe cleaner
- ❑ 4 thread spools, film canisters, or corks
- ❑ tempera or acrylic paints, or felt-tip pens
- ❑ paintbrushes
- ❑ white glue
- ❑ pencil
- ❑ scissors
- ❑ paper hole punch
- ❑ an adult

1. Make a drawing of the pig's head on cardboard, including the tabs, as shown. Then, cut it out.

2. Cut a 1 1/4 inch slit at the side of one bowl.

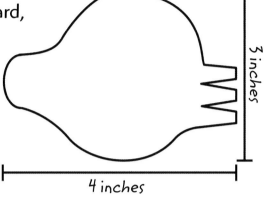

3 inches

4 inches

3. Slide the head into the slit and bend out the tabs and glue them to the inside of the bowl, as shown.

4. Punch a small hole in the bowl on the side opposite the head and insert a curled pipe cleaner as a tail. Glue or tape the pipe cleaner to the inside of the bowl to secure it.

5. Have an adult cut a slot in the center of the pig's back, large enough for a quarter to fall through (about 1/4 inch wide and 1 1/2 inches long).

6. To make the body, apply glue to the rim of the other bowl and put the bowl with the pig's head directly on it, as shown. Let them dry.

7. To make legs, glue four thread spools to the bottom of the pig. Let them dry.

8. Paint your pig and add a snout and other features.

Butterfly Magnet

Here is one butterfly that won't fly away! Use this magnet to hold special papers and pictures on your refrigerator.

What you'll need

- ☐ miniature clothespin
- ☐ tissue paper
- ☐ adhesive magnetic tape
- ☐ pipe cleaners
- ☐ glue
- ☐ scissors

1. Cut three pieces of tissue paper into 3-inch squares.

2. Gather one square in the middle and clip the clothespin around it, as shown.

3. Repeat step 2 with the other two pieces of tissue paper, overlapping the pieces.

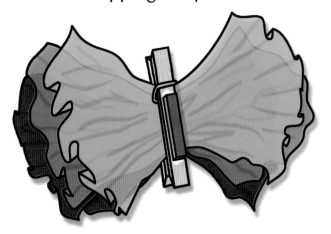

4. Put several drops of glue on the clothespin to hold the tissue paper in place. Be careful not to rip the tissue paper when you open the clothespin.

5. Cut a piece of magnetic tape to glue to the back of the butterfly, as shown.

6. Twist pipe cleaners around the top of the clothespin to form the antennae.

Suggestion

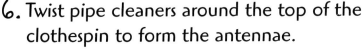

- Have an adult use hot glue to make it last longer.

Treasure Box

Design your own special box that opens and closes. Use it to hold your favorite treasures!

What you'll need

- [ ] 2 disposable soup bowls
- [ ] hairpin or twisty tie
- [ ] crayons, felt-tip pens, watercolors, tempera or acrylic paints
- [ ] white glue
- [ ] small round button or bead
- [ ] paper hole punch
- [ ] decorative stickers, glitter, ribbon, etc. (optional)

Here's how . . .

1. To make a hinged box, punch two holes about 1 inch apart through the rims of the two bowls.

2. Thread a hairpin through each pair of holes and twist the ends to make it secure, as shown.

3. Decorate the box. Use an idea shown here or create your own design.

4. Add stickers or other decorations, if desired.

5. Glue the button to the front of the lid to make opening and closing easier.

Plate Mirror

Every face needs a mirror. Use colored yarn to match your room!

What you'll need

- [ ] 1 sturdy 9" paper plate
- [ ] 1 round mirror, not more than 5 inches in diameter (across)
- [ ] yarn in different colors
- [ ] glue
- [ ] paper clip
- [ ] scissors
- [ ] toothpick
- [ ] pencil
- [ ] sponge

1. Glue the mirror to the center of the paper plate and let it dry.

2. Make a colorful border around the plate by gluing yarn to the rim. Use a toothpick to press and guide the yarn. Cut the yarn where the ends meet and press them together.

3. In the same way as step 2, glue yarn around the edge of the mirror, so that the mirror's edges are covered, as shown.

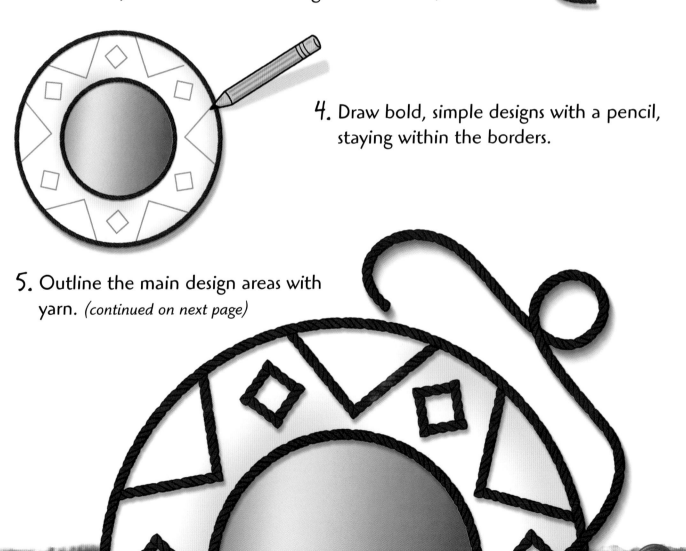

4. Draw bold, simple designs with a pencil, staying within the borders.

5. Outline the main design areas with yarn. *(continued on next page)*

6. Fill in the small areas, one at a time, by winding a single piece of yarn inward from the border to the center. Use a variety of colors to fill it in. Apply glue as you need it. Use a clean damp sponge to remove any extra glue. Continue doing this until the plate is completely covered with yarn.

7. When dry, attach a paper clip to the back of the plate for hanging, as shown.

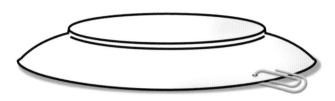

Suggestion

● Have an adult use hot glue to make it last longer.